I THAT WAS BORN IN WALES

I THAT WAS BORN IN WALES

A New Selection from the Poems of
VERNON WATKINS

Chosen and Introduced by
Gwen Watkins and Ruth Pryor

CARDIFF
UNIVERSITY OF WALES PRESS
1976

© Gwen Watkins, 1976

ISBN 0 7083 0615 2

Printed by the John Penry Press, Swansea

"I that was born in Wales
Cherish heaven's dust in scales
Which may at dusk be seen
On every village green
Where Tawe, Taff or Wye
Through fields and woods goes by . . ."

From The Death Bell

CONTENTS

CONTENTS

FOREWORD

Vernon Watkins was born at Maesteg, Glamorgan, in 1906. He came to Swansea at the age of six, and moved soon after to Gower, where he lived most of his life. He was educated at Repton and Magdalene College, Cambridge, and worked as a clerk in Lloyds Bank from the age of twenty-three until his retirement at sixty. During the 1939-45 war he served in the Royal Air Force. After his retirement from the Bank he became the first Gulbenkian Fellow in Poetry at the University College of Swansea in 1966. He died in Seattle in 1967, while he was Visiting Professor of Poetry at the University of Washington.

He received many honours during his lifetime. He was elected Fellow of the Royal Society of Literature in 1951, won the first Guinness Prize for Poetry in 1957, was twice awarded the Travelling Fellowship of the Society of Authors, in 1952 and 1956, and was made an Honorary D.Litt. of the University of Wales in 1966. Faber and Faber published seven books of poems: *The Ballad of the Mari Lwyd*, 1941; *The Lamp and the Veil*, 1945; *The Lady with the Unicorn*, 1948; *The Death Bell*, 1954; *Cypress and Acacia*, 1959; *Affinities*, 1962; *Fidelities* (published posthumously), 1968. A further volume of *Uncollected Poems* was prepared after his death and published by the Enitharmon Press in 1969; another posthumous collection of poems is still to come from the Enitharmon Press. Faber brought out a volume of translations from Heine, *The North Sea*, in 1951, and a further collection of translations mainly from French and German poets is to be published by the Enitharmon Press, together with a volume of selected prose pieces. A volume of letters from Dylan Thomas, *Letters to Vernon Watkins*, edited by himself, was brought out by Dent and Faber in 1957, and a collection of letters from David Jones is to be published by the University of Wales Press. Two volumes of *Selected Poems* were published in the poet's lifetime, an American one in 1948 by New Directions, the other by Faber in 1967. Two notable books on Vernon Watkins have appeared; a memorial volume edited by Leslie Norris, *Vernon Watkins 1906-1967* (Faber and Faber, 1970); and *Vernon Watkins* by Roland Mathias (University of Wales Press, 1974).

The poems in this new selection are arranged according to their themes, the themes that were of paramount importance to Vernon Watkins as a poet. The poems have been taken from among those we consider his best. The book is not intended to be a representative selection of his work; we have included none of his ballads and few of the well-known anthology pieces. It is intended to introduce his poetry to new readers, and to give those who already know his work a selection of poems which not only form a unity in themselves, but which throw light on one another.

We have had to choose from a very large *oeuvre*, and so have not been able to include everything we should have liked to include. We have confined ourselves to the themes which seem to be at the heart of the poetry: Wales, Dylan Thomas, Poetry and the Poet, Life and Death. Wales was the place in which he grew, and Dylan Thomas the poet who was his closest friend. Vernon Watkins is one of the few poets since Wordsworth who have written much about what it means to be a poet. Although he believed that he would, like Yeats, write his greatest poetry in old age, his Muse knew better; and so we have added a short final section which contains poems he wrote in the last years of his life which seem to anticipate his death.

The poet's own words best express the principle which lay behind all his work, and on which this selection is based:

I am convinced that the foundation of art is joy. In the visual arts, in poetry and music, the act of creation is joy. This is true, whether the work is tragic or gay or even bitter. Certainly this creative joy is of a unique kind. One might think that the artists who are given it should be happy, but often they are not. There is a tension between their own values and those of the world, there is often poverty, there is the failure to satisfy the demands of their own imagination, the gulf between desire and achievement, but in spite of these, in the act of creative work, an artist is, and always has been, drawing from joy.

The quality and intensity of a work depends on the sensibility of the artist. A masterpiece is never exhausted.

First of all, it is always fresh; it renews itself continuously, it is always beginning. There is also this about it, that it cannot be repeated. If we were to go back four or five centuries we might overhear an artist say this to himself:

'What I owe I owe to the Past. But one thing I do not owe to the Past: the gift or accident which makes my work my own, so that it cannot be repeated.'

Far from believing that an artist should not repeat himself, I believe that he should make what cannot be repeated by others. Repetition may be a reinforcement of the individual will, even a statement of faith, and that is sacred. Unless there is a constant and a recurrence, there is no depth in the matrix.

(From a note preserved among the personal papers of Vernon Watkins).

GWEN WATKINS
RUTH PRYOR.

Pennard, November 1975.

Wales

INTRODUCTION

I am a Welsh poet writing in English. I dislike the term 'Anglo-Welsh' because it immediately suggests a mixed parentage. There are many poets with one Welsh parent and one English, but I am, like Dylan Thomas, entirely Welsh by birth, and I believe that my verse is characteristically Welsh in the same way that the verse of Yeats is characteristically Irish. The use of English by Welsh or Irish or Scottish poets is bound to be different in certain ways, because rhythm and cadence are born in the blood. In a political writer, especially in one who feels that his own people are oppressed, nationality is betrayed by protest, by what is said. I am not a political writer. I am entirely concerned with metaphysical truth.

These were the words Vernon Watkins used to introduce a reading of his poems at Gregynog in 1967. He was of completely Welsh descent, was born in Wales, and lived most of his life in Wales. His father's family came from Taff's Well in Glamorgan; his mother was a Phillips from Carmarthen, and for both his parents Welsh was their first language. Vernon Watkins himself could not speak Welsh, and could read the language only with a dictionary. He called himself 'a Welsh poet writing in English.' After his University days he seldom left Wales except to do his war service; when he did leave, it was on short visits and holidays. He lived in Gower from the age of twelve, and although he died in the United States, he was at the time on leave of absence from his Gulbenkian Fellowship at the University College of Swansea.

A large number of his poems are on Welsh themes. His first book had as its title poem, 'The Ballad of the Mari Lwyd', based on the ancient Welsh New Year's custom, and the first two poems in it were 'The Collier' and 'Sonnet (Pit Boy)'. He was still writing poems about Wales and Gower when he died; some of them have been published since his death. In all his books of poems there are poems about Wales..

Although he disliked being called a nature poet, many of his metaphysical poems have their beginning in the landscape of Wales: the several Taliesin poems, 'Rhossili', 'Ode to Swansea', 'The Red Lady' (of Paviland), 'The Ballad of Hunt's Bay', 'Returning to Goleufryn'.

Among his friends were many Welsh artists, in his own and other arts: Dylan Thomas, R. S. Thomas, David Jones, Idris Davies and many others.

Waterfalls

Always in that valley in Wales I hear the noise
Of waters falling.
              There is a clump of trees
  We climbed for nuts; and high in the trees the boys
    Lost in the rookery's cries
      Would cross, and branches cracking under their knees

Would break, and make in the winter wood new gaps.
 The leafmould covering the ground was almost black,
  But speckled and striped were the nuts we threw in our caps,
   Milked from split shells and cups,
    Secret as chestnuts when they are tipped from a sack,

Glossy and new.
             Always in that valley in Wales
I hear that sound, those voices. They keep fresh
  What ripens, falls, drops into darkness, fails,
   Gone when dawn shines on scales,
    And glides from village memory, slips through the mesh,

And is not, when we come again.
                I look:
Voices are under the bridge, and that voice calls,
  Now late, and answers;
              then, as the light twigs break
  Back, there is only the brook
   Reminding the stones where, under a breath, it falls.

From: *The Broken Sea*

My lamp that was lit every night has burnt a hole in the
    shade.
A seawave plunges. Listen. Below me crashes the bay.
The rushing greedy water smothers the talk of the spade.
Now, on the sixth of November, I remember the tenth of
    May.

I was going to fly to your christening to give you a cup.
Here, like Andersen's tailor, I weave the invisible thread.
The burnt-out clock of St. Mary's has come to a stop,
And the hand still points to the figure that beckons the
    house-stoned dead.

Child Shades of my ignorant darkness, I mourn that moment
    alive
Near the glow-lamped Eumenides' house, overlooking the
    ships in flight,
Where Pearl White focussed our childhood, near the foot of
    Cwmdonkin Drive,
To a figment of crime stampeding in the posters' wind-blown
    blight.

I regret the broken Past, its prompt and punctilious cares,
All the villainies of the fire-and-brimstone-visited town.
I miss the painter of limbo at the top of the fragrant stairs,
The extravagant hero of night, his iconoclastic frown.

Through the criminal thumb-prints of soot, in the
    swaddling-bands of a shroud,
I pace the familiar street, and the wall repeats my pace,
Alone in the blown-up city, lost in a bird-voiced crowd
Murdered where shattering breakers at your pillow's head
    leave lace.

For death has burst upon you, yet your light-flooded eyes do
    not tremble
Where pictures for waking life stand in the spray's wild bead.
You are guarded, shrined in the torrent, fast-locked in the cave
    of the Sibyl,
In that terrifying delay of the waters' magical speed.

Asleep to-night in Paris, not knowing I walk your world,
You are deaf to the schoolyard's voices, where, escaped, the
    children meet,
The world of a child's one town, renascent, in rage unfurled
Between Cwmdonkin railing and black-faced Inkerman
    Street.

Waves, hooded, raging, thunder, hiding contagious guilt,
Tossing, high on the shale, the hard and scribbled stones.
An anchor's dirge is buried under the waters' quilt.
Dazzling sunbeams have hidden the hook and the barnacled
    bones.

O indifferent grains of sand, O mother-of-pearl of the shell,
I hear the inconstant water, the blind, the wandering one.
The groan of Sophocles, and the groan of the leper's bell
Burst on annhilation: through your window breaks the sun.

I hear the breath of the storm. The engulfed, Gargantuan tide
Heaped in hills by the moles, hurls to the mountain's head
The streets of sunrise, O windows burning on Townhill side,
O light of annunciation, unearthing the unknown dead!

The Forge of the Solstice

The best are older: with the unrest time brings,
No absolute remains to bind them fast.
One scrawls on rock the names of hallowed things,
Letters and hieroglyphs that yet shall last
When darkness measures with a martyr's eye
The glories shed by life's unchanging tree.

Another, curbing vigour on his page
To movement, makes the abounding life his own
And rhythmic finds in a discordant age,
Singing like living fountains sprung from stone,
Those unifying harmonies of line
Torn from creative nature. Light is born

Under believing fingers. Men refute
By inward protest what their masters teach,
Seeking a deeper meaning. One is mute,
Fearing far more the heresies of speech
Than watchful waiting. Figures move; they pass
Across the cave. Before them flies heaven's glass,

And out of it now falls the winter sun,
Leaving a ceaseless myth of moving waves,
Till darkness quiets all things. Man is one:
The identity survives its many graves.
First was the hunter, then the prophet; last,
The artificer, compounding in one ghost

Hunter and prey, prophet and witness, brought
Into that circle where all riddles end.
Love gives their art a body in which thought
Draws, not from time but wisdom, till it bend
The solstice like a bow, and bring time round
White with young stars, quick from the forge they have
        found.

Peace in the Welsh Hills

Calm is the landscape when the storm has passed,
Brighter the fields, and fresh with fallen rain.
Where gales beat out new colour from the hills
Rivers fly faster, and upon their banks
Birds preen their wings, and irises revive.
Not so the cities burnt alive with fire
Of man's destruction: when their smoke is spent,
No phoenix rises from the ruined walls.

I ponder now the grief of many rooms.
Was it a dream, that age, when fingers found
A satisfaction sleeping in dumb stone,
When walls were built responding to the touch
In whose high gables, in the lengthening days,
Martins would nest? Though crops, though lives, would fail,
Though friends dispersed, unchanged the walls would stay,
And still those wings return to build in Spring.

Here, where the earth is green, where heaven is true
Opening the windows, touched with earliest dawn,
In the first frost of cool September days,
Chrysanthemum weather, presaging great birth,
Who in his heart could murmur or complain:
'The light we look for is not in this land?'
That light is present, and that distant time
Is always here, continually redeemed.

There is a city we must build with joy
Exactly where the fallen city sleeps.
There is one road through village, town and field,
On whose robust foundation Chaucer dreamed
A ride could wed the opposites in man.
There proud walls may endure, and low walls feed
The imagination if they have a vine
Or shadowy barn made rich with gathered corn.

Great mansions fear from their surrounding trees
The invasion of a wintry desolation
Filling their rooms with leaves. And cottages
Bring the sky down as flickering candles do,
Leaning on their own shadows. I have seen
Vases and polished brass reflect black windows
And draw the ceiling down to their vibrations,
Thick, deep, and white-washed, like a bank of snow.

To live entwined in pastoral loveliness
May rest the eyes, throw pictures on the mind,
But most we need a metaphor of stone
Such as those painters had whose mountain-cities
Cast long, low shadows on the Umbrian hills.
There, in some courtyard on the cobbled stone,
A fountain plays, and through a cherub's mouth
Ages are linked by water in the sunlight.

All of good faith that fountain may recall,
Woman, musician, boy, or else a scholar
Reading a Latin book. They seem distinct,
And yet are one, because tranquillity
Affirms the Judgement. So, in these Welsh hills,
I marvel, waking from a dream of stone,
That such a peace surrounds me, while the city
For which all long has never yet been built.

The Return of Spring

The Spring returns. Green valleys, the sparkling meadows
Crowd gold, under larks, wry-rooted, the gorse, deep-scented.
Lovely it is to live, to turn the eyes seaward,
To laugh with waves that outlive us.

And marvellously the sundering, receding seawaves
Pound the resounding sands; they knock at the hour-glass.
Thunder compels no man, yet a thought compels him,
Lost, neglected, yet tender.

Why in the wood, where already the new leaves mending
Winter's wild net, cast fragile, immature shadows,
Do I tread pure darkness, resisting that green dominion?
What is the thing more sacred?

Taut branches exude gold wax of the breaking buds.
Sweet finches sing. The stream has a hundred voices
Unheard before. One leans on the grass like a bridegroom,
And death slips under the bride-sleep.

Wait for no second Spring in Bishopston Valley.
Once, once only it breaks. If you plunge your fingers
In the stream, all secrets under the Earth grow articulate
In a moment, and for you only.

Diamonds of light, emeralds of leaves, green jewels:
For me the unnoticed, death-touching script is more
          passionate.
Cover the tome with dust; there dwells the redeemer,
Deathlessly known by the voice-fall.

O Spring, the box of colours, blue sky, green trees!
Has the brook ears? Donne has delivered his sermon.
Not easily you beguile the pulse, the footprint
Vaulted with intimate music.

Yet you return, bring beauty to Earth. I see
The skill and wonder you practise upon our eyes.
Break the veiled branches. Still, in the single leaf
It holds you, silken, a garland.

O returning child, not knowing why you were born,
Not understanding world's beauty the dead sustain,
The sharpness of colour, the clearness of water are yours;
The love there shadowed you know not.

What first I feared as a rite I love as a sacrament.
The Spring returns. I look. There is no dissembling.
The brook falters, runs on. I divine those meanings,
Listening to tongues that are silent.

Bishopston Stream

River last seen in Spring, you race in the light of Autumn.
Now, as you run through hazels, their leaves are already
    falling.
Out of the wood I come, astonished again to find you
Younger and swifter.

There were two voices then, moving about in foliage.
One called the other voice, then a great bird made silence.
This was their meeting-place, here where the heron paddling
Stepped on the square stone.

Crossing an open space, haunted in June by mayflies,
Into the gloom of trees you wind through Bishopston Valley,
Darting, kingfisher-blue, carrying a streak of silver
Fished from oblivion.

Over your tunnelled song, pulled in the year's declining,
Lies an uprooted elm, struck by a gale or lightning.
Trout in the shadows hide; black is the hurrying water,
Thronged once with Spring stars.

May not the two I saw be in this hour united
Who are gone different ways? Water, that young Rebecca,
Naomi, Ruth, once heard, voices above a pitcher,
Late let me stoop here.

Yet if I listen closely, singing of separation,
Singing of night you go, through a continual darkness,
River of exile's voice, harps that were hung heard plainly
Now, in the clear dusk.

Even by day you run through a continual darkness.
Could we interpret time, we should be like the angels.
Always against your sound there is a second river
Speaks, by its silence.

Poetry and the Poet

INTRODUCTION

WHAT THE POET SAYS

I am a lyric poet. I also believe that the sound-pattern of lyric poetry is more closely related to music than to prose. Do not misunderstand me. Some of the purest lines in poetry are colloquial speech, that is to say, they would not be at all out of place in prose; but the dominant pattern of any poem that is lyrical is totally different, and this is, even mathematically, closer to music than to prose.

Poetry that is divorced from living speech, and by this I mean the speech-idiom of to-day, runs a great risk of being artificial, and therefore losing its power to move. Even so, if his theme demands it, a poet must take this risk. Poetry is, after all, artificial in structure; it is artifice; and the poet who believes only in the order of natural speech will neglect that other, compelling order, the order of imaginative emphasis.

I believe that lyric poetry is closer to music than to prose, and that it should be read as exactly as a musical score. I also believe that it is always a gift, the reward of tenacity and minutest attention, and that unless it comes out of exaltation or moves towards it, it is not worth writing.

I suppose every writer, in applauding another's work, undergoes a modulation of sensibility, but I cannot see how any poet whose roots are deep can be fundamentally influenced by a living contemporary. I never think a true style can be learnt from contemporaries.

A good poem is one that can never be fashionable. What is fresh must also be ancient, and a poem is not finished until it attains its most ancient form. The more ancient a poem is, the more modern it becomes; and will remain so, when apparent modernity is obsolete.

I am not a nature poet, nor a descriptive poet. Of course I write about nature, the well of inexhaustible secrets, and of course I describe, but nature and description are not as necessary to my imagination as the presentation of paradoxical truth. The corrective matters more to me than the spontaneous. I go further. The corrective is closer to inspiration because it employs the full range of perception. It is spontaneity in its second pressure; it is spontaneity plus. The indefinable quality that is added is poetry, the poem's truth. It is the secret that ordinary, unattended appreciation could never achieve.

I consider destructive criticism worthless, so far as poetry is concerned, and evaluative criticism worthless, too. Out of the vast body of poetry that exists I recommend you to read what you like most. Read one poet at a time. If you read in an anthology, separate the poet you are reading from the others, if necessary by keeping your hand over the opposite page. Poetry deserves concentration, and it cannot get this in an anthology where different talents jostle about for a place in your mind. Read the poem you like several times, and read it aloud.

The will is a daemonic thing, and it is through the will that a poet chooses.

The will is very important, but alone it can do nothing, for the instinct of the will is to move in one direction, and creation is never in a straight line.

The will of a poet is like a hawk hovering, about to fall, caught up again into the clouds by the complexity of his own desire. What he must trust is his instinct for truth.

Life, in all its variegated and sometimes contradictory patterns, is spread out before him. The will, before it chooses, must be suspended, sometimes for a very long period. In lyric poetry the choice, the moment of resolution, depends on the intervention of luck. Order and luck define the poem.

However long a work of poetry takes, composition is always a swift, a lightning thing; and even Goethe's *Faust*, which took over fifty years to finish, is bound to carry, here and there, the marks of hurried composition, because it is the work of a poet. What mattered to the poet was not the time taken over the work, but the demands it made on him. Those demands communicate a tension which the reader shares; he needs, for a true understanding of the poetry, a vicarious experience of composition. In his mind he writes the poem.

(Extracts from notes used by Vernon Watkins for teaching poetry, and for introducing his public poetry readings, and preserved among his personal papers at the time of his death).

Rewards of the Fountain

Let the world offer what it will,
Its bargains I refuse.
Those it rewards are greedy still.
I serve a stricter Muse.

She bears no treasure but the sands,
No bounty but the sea's.
The fountain falls on empty hands.
She only gives to these.

The living water sings through her
Whose eyes are fixed on stone.
My strength is from the sepulchre
Where time is overthrown.

If once I labour to possess
A gift that is not hers,
The more I gain in time, the less
I triumph in the verse.

Demands of the Muse

I call up words that he may write them down.
My falling into labour gives him birth.
My sorrows are not sorrows till he weeps.
I learn from him as much as he from me
Who is my chosen and my tool in time.

I am dumb: my burden is not like another.
My lineaments are hid from him who knows me.
Great is my Earth with undelivered words.
It is my dead, my dead, that sing to him
This ancient moment; and their voice is he.

Born into time of love's perceptions, he
Is not of time. The acts of time to him
Are marginal. From the first hour he knows me
Until the last, he shall divine my words.
In his own solitude he hears another.

I make demands of him more than another.
He sets himself a labour built of words
Which, through my lips, brings sudden joy to him.
He has the illusion that at last he knows me.
When the toil ends, my confidant is he.

Vision makes wise at once. Why then must he
Wait through so many years before he knows me?
The bit is tempered to restrain his words
And make laborious all that's dear to him.
So he remains himself and not another.

Why is he slow to praise me when another
Falls at my feet? What conscience moves in him
To make a stubborn stand before he knows me?
It is reluctance that resolves his words.
I have been cursed, indeed, by such as he.

Yet, though a school invoke me, it is he
I choose, for opposition gives those words
Their strength; and there is none more near to him
In thought. It is by conflict that he knows me
And serves me in my way and not another.

C—IBW

Demands of the Poet

I set my heart against all lesser toil.
Speak to me now more closely than the birds.
That labour done, on which I spent my oil,
Avails me nothing till you test the words.

How much the beating pulse may hold the years
Yet write the athletic wisdom on the page
You alone say. You bring the authentic tears
Which recognize the moment without age.

No lesser vision gives me consolation.
Wealth is a barren waste, that spring forgot.
Art is the principle of all creation,
And there the desert is, where art is not.

The Interval

This now being finished and the next unknown,
I must wait long to find the words I need.
Verse tests the very marrow in the bone,
Yet man, being once engaged by song, is freed:
The act itself is prayer, deliberate in its speed.

Nature needs waste; even friendship needs a gap.
Wines love delay and boats a measured stroke.
Distance divides lightning and thunderclap,
Yet time can in a crystal cleared of smoke
Show Earth's arrested lives in mute, transparent cloak.

Now by what current is the swimmer borne
Feeling its pull and subterranean force?
Are the dead parched, or hunger the unborn
For present music, that its certain course
Alone may fill their need and heal them of remorse?

No pressure from this upper ground compels.
It is that dark source which makes all things new
Scoops out, with changing lights, those fragile shells
Whose voice would perish, did I not pursue
Their inmost labyrinth still, to give the god his due.

Vine

Deep-rooted vine, delay your fruit
Beyond youth's rashness. I have seen
Rich promise wither to the root
Before its time had been.

Drain all the darkness of the soil
And stand there shrivelled, crisp and dry,
Too lifeless in your parchment coil
To open one green eye.

Some watch the March winds animate
Those early bulbs in Winter's bed.
Envy them not, but keep your state.
Let others think you dead.

Contain in secrecy that balm
Strengthening the sap before it move,
That the broad leaves from wells of calm
One day grow dark with love.

I know a tree as dry as yours.
The patient leaf is put forth late.
Its life is anchored in the hours
For which the heart must wait.

The Heron

The cloud-backed heron will not move:
He stares into the stream.
He stands unfaltering while the gulls
And oyster-catchers scream.
He does not hear, he cannot see
The great white horses of the sea,
But fixes eyes on stillness
Below their flying team.

How long will he remain, how long
Have the grey woods been green?
The sky and the reflected sky,
Their glass he has not seen,
But silent as a speck of sand
Interpreting the sea and land,
His fall pulls down the fabric
Of all that windy scene.

Sailing with clouds and woods behind,
Pausing in leisured flight,
He stepped, alighting on a stone,
Dropped from the stars of night.
He stood there unconcerned with day,
Deaf to the tumult of the bay,
Watching a stone in water,
A fish's hidden light.

Sharp rocks drive back the breaking waves,
Confusing sea with air.
Bundles of spray blown mountain-high
Have left the shingle bare.
A shipwrecked anchor wedged by rocks,
Loosed by the thundering equinox,
Divides the herded waters,
The stallion and his mare.

Yet no distraction breaks the watch
Of that time-killing bird.
He stands unmoving on the stone;
Since dawn he has not stirred.
Calamity about him cries,
But he has fixed his golden eyes
On water's crooked tablet,
On light's reflected word.

Swan Narcissus

Snared in the rustling sheath of winter,
Neck high in March, not yet remembering
Water-notes near the nape attentive,
How like a swan the narcissus opens.

Slow the ascent, compact the statement,
Patient the shell, still shut forever,
Stubborn against the beat of sunlight
Falling in waves of its own divining.

This, as the star knows night, knows earthspring.
Torn from the husk and coil of seasons,
Sprung from dark earth, in the air it rises,
Printing on time its eternal pattern.

How like a wing that single petal
Breaks from the gold eye fixed on darkness,
Born like the solitary to stillness,
Praising alone what surpasses nature.

Taliesin and the Spring of Vision

'I tread the sand at the sea's edge, sand of the hour-glass,
And the sand receives my footprint, singing:
"You are my nearmost, you who have travelled the farthest,
And you are my constant, who have endured all vicissitudes
In the cradle of sea, Fate's hands, and the spinning waters.
The measure of past grief is the measure of present joy.
Your tears, which have dried to Chance, now spring from a
    secret.
Here time's glass breaks, and the world is transfigured in
    music." '

So sang the grains of sand, and while they whirled to a pattern
Taliesin took refuge under the unfledged rock.
He could not see in the cave, but groped with his hand,
And the rock he touched was the socket of all men's eyes,
And he touched the spring of vision. He had the mind of a fish
That moment. He knew the glitter of scale and fin.
He touched the pin of pivotal space, and he saw
One sandgrain balance the ages' cumulus cloud.

Earth's shadow hung. Taliesin said: 'The penumbra of history
    is terrible.
Life changes, breaks, scatters. There is no sheet-anchor.
Time reigns; yet the kingdom of love is every moment,
Whose citizens do not age in each other's eyes.
In a time of darkness the pattern of life is restored
By men who make all transience seem an illusion
Through inward acts, acts corresponding to music.
Their works of love leave words that do not end in the heart.'

He still held rock. Then three drops fell on his fingers,
And Future and Past converged in a lightning flash:
'It was we who instructed Shakespeare, who fell upon
    Dante's eyes,
Who opened to Blake the Minute Particulars. We are the
    soul's rebirth.'

Taliesin answered: 'I have encountered the irreducible
        diamond
In the rock. Yet now it is over. Omniscience is not for man.
Christen me, therefore, that my acts in the dark may be just,
And adapt my partial vision to the limitation of time.'

Muse, Poet and Fountain

No living man may compass what I seek.
No eye outside my own may judge these things;
And mine are downcast that my hand may speak.
In me tears end; from me the fountain springs.

Though time still falls from future into past,
Nothing is gone my hand may not restore.
Mine is the pulse that makes your pulse beat fast,
Harmonious joy with stillness at the core.

I am your peace, wherever fortune move you,
Your strength, your birthright and your native ground.
I wait to give, whether men scorn or love you,
Prodigal strength, returning to my sound.
Not while you live, but when grass waves above you,
When you are dead, your labour shall be crowned.

Dylan Thomas

INTRODUCTION

Vernon Watkins and Dylan Thomas first met soon after the publication of 18 *Poems* in December 1934. Their meeting is described in the introduction to *Letters to Vernon Watkins:*

> He was slight, shorter than I had expected, shy, rather flushed and eager in manner, deep-voiced, restless, humorous, with large, wondering, yet acutely intelligent eyes, gold curls, snub nose, and the face of a cherub. I quickly realised when we went for a walk on the cliffs that this cherub took nothing for granted. In thought and words he was anarchic, challenging, with the certainty of that instinct which knows its own freshly discovered truth.
>
> We became close friends almost immediately, from an affinity which I think we both recognised at once. That affinity was particularly clear when we talked about poetry or read it aloud; yet our approach to it and our way of working presented a complete contrast. Dylan worked upon a symmetrical abstract with tactile delicacy; out of a lump of texture or nest of phrases he created music, testing everything by physical feeling, working from the concrete image outwards. I worked from music and cadence towards the density of physical shape. I worked at night, he in the day, usually in the afternoon, but never in the evening which he regarded as the social time of the day. I used titles; he did not; but I did eventually persuade him to use them. At first he saw no reason why a poet should use a title any more than a composer, and he disliked what seemed to him an unnecessary label of simplification. Later, the title itself was able to give him a measure of excitement without which the measure of the poem would be incomplete.
>
> My first impression of a rooted obstinacy, which was really a rooted innocence, was reinforced whenever we met. We met often, either at his house or mine.

Dylan's home was in Cwmdonkin Drive, Swansea, and Vernon's at Pennard on the Gower Peninsula, about eight miles away. Whenever they met they would read and discuss poetry: their own, each other's, and the poetry of other poets. When Dylan moved to Laugharne they met in Laugharne, Pennard or Swansea, and later, during the War, in London.

Dylan's death in November 1953 was a grief from which Vernon never recovered. One of his sons, born in April 1954, was named after Dylan, who was to have been his godfather (see 'Birth and Morning' in *Cypress and Acacia*). Vernon wrote many poems about Dylan, but only three, 'Portrait of a Friend' (*The Ballad of the Mari Lwyd*), the part of 'The Broken Sea' (*The Lamp and the Veil*) which refers to Dylan, and 'Sailors on the Moving Land' (*Life and Letters*, 1949), were written in his lifetime. All the others were written after his death: five in *Cypress and Acacia*—'The Sloe', 'The Return', 'The Exacting Ghost', 'The Curlew' and 'Buried Light';

one, 'A True Picture Restored', in *Affinities*; five more in *Fidelities*—
'Exegesis', 'The Snow Curlew', 'At Cwmrhydyceirw Quarry', 'To a Shell',
'Cwmrhydyceirw Elegiacs'; and 'Elegy for the Latest Dead', a sequence
of five sonnets first published in *Botteghe Oscure* in 1954. 'A True Pic-
ture Restored' seems the most complete statement of what Dylan Thomas
meant to Vernon Watkins and of his importance to poetry and to Wales.
It is omitted from this selection only for reasons of space. The best
record of the personal and poetic relationship of the two men is the Dylan
Thomas *Letters to Vernon Watkins* (Dent and Faber, 1957).

The Curlew

Sweet-throated cry, by one no longer heard
Who, more than many, loved the wandering bird,
Unchanged through generations and renewed,
Perpetual child of its own solitude,
The same on rocks and over sea I hear
Return now with his unreturning year.
How swiftly now it flies across the sands,
Image of change unchanging, changing lands
From year to year, yet always found near home
Where waves in sunlight break in restless foam.
Old though the cave is, this outlives the cave,
And the grey pool that shuddered when it gave
The landscape life, reveals where time has grown,
Turning green, slowly forming tears to stone.
The quick light of that cry disturbs the gloom.
It passes now, and rising from its tomb,
Carries remorse across the sea where I
Wait on the shore, still listening to that cry
Which bears a ghostly listening to my own;
Such life is hidden in the ringing stone
That rests, unmatched by any natural thing,
And joins, unheard, the wave-crest and the wing.

Exegesis

So many voices
Instead of one.
Light, that is the driving force
Of song alone:
Give me this or darkness,
The man or his bone.

None shall replace him,
Only falsify
Light broken into colours,
The altered sky.
Hold back the bridle,
Or the truth will lie.

The Sloe

Too like those lineaments
For waking eyes to see,
Yet those the dream presents
Clearly to me.

How much more vivid now
Than when across your tomb
Sunlight projects a bough
In gradual gloom!

Even such a curious taste
I found, seeing Winter blow
Above a leafless waste
The bitter sloe.

It will not yet begin
To act upon the tongue
Till tooth has pierced the skin
And juice has sprung:

A flavour tart and late
Which, when the rest had gone,
Could hide in mist and wait,
Its roots in stone.

The Present

Strange, is it not, that he for whom
The living moment stood in flesh,
Should bring the future to this room
Held at arm's length, and always fresh.

Strange, that his echoing words can spell
New meanings though the die is cast,
And tell us more than time can tell,
Immediate in a timeless Past;

And stranger still, for us who knew
The living face and now return
Its pictured gaze, so quick, so new,
Love's vital fire being its concern,

To think, though years should gallop now
Or lag behind, he will not care,
So calm the eyes beneath the brow,
Held in a breath by angels there.

Cwmrhydyceirw Elegiacs

Go, swallow, and tell, now that the summer is dying,
Spirits who loved him in time, where in the earth he is laid.
Dumb secrets are here, hard as the elm-roots in winter;
We who are left here confront words of inscrutable calm.
Life cuts into stone this that on earth is remembered,
How for the needs of the dead loving provision was made.
Strong words remain true, under the hammer of Babel:
Sleeps in the heart of the rock all that a god would restore.

Never shall time be stilled in the quarry of Cwmrhydyceirw,
Not while the boulder recoils under the force of the fuse.
Tablets imprisoned by rock, inert in the sleeping arena,
Quake in the shudder of air, knowing the swallow has passed.
One grief is enough, one tongue, to transfigure the ages:
Let our tears for the dead earn the forgiveness of dust.

Buried Light

What are the light and wind to me?
The lamp I love is gone to ground.
There all the thunder of the sea
Becomes by contrast idle sound.

What hammer on the anvil falls?
Who shapes the cyclone to his will?
The moments and the intervals
Gain their estate from what is still.

All hunting opposites I praise.
I praise the falcon and the dove.
Night's intense darkness gives to days
True pictures of regenerate love.

Come, buried light, and honour time
With your dear gift, your constancy,
That the known world be made sublime
Through visions that closed eyelids see.

Come, breath, instruct this angry wind
To listen here where men have prayed,
That the bold landscape of the mind
Fly nobler from its wrist of shade.

Sons of true sacrifice are there.
Rivers and hills are in their hands.
The lightest petal the winds bear
Has mocked the Serpent's swaddling-bands.

And men may find beneath the sun,
Dashed into pieces by old wrong,
A relic, lost to nature, one
Whose passion stops the mouth of song.

To a Shell

At last, beautiful shell,
Lie there crushed; but the sea
Cannot obliterate yet
Faith I remember well:
A house facing the sea.
Hard and bitterly
Though waves beat on that wall
From the swirling quicksands of debt,
I swear that it cannot fall.

Nor can you drag those words,
Confident in their day,
Down to the unknown deep.
I have a net whose cords
Gather the fallen day
And make the forgotten stay
In all but the detail death
Moves to the realm of sleep,
So strong is the pledge of breath.

And though the magical dice,
Loaded for nothing, toss
All to perdition, left
In darkness, held in a vice,
No white breaker can toss
All to a total loss.
Still the relic will hold,
Caught in a secret cleft,
Tenderer light than gold.

All I remember, all
Of the locked, unfolding days
Where to-morrow's treasure shines.
Fragile nautilus caul,
Tell the fingers of days:
'Find me. Enter the praise
Of Eden's morning, inlaid
With dazzling, intimate lines.
Touch, and the world will fade.'

The Snow Curlew

Snow has fallen all night
Over the cliff. There are no paths.
All is even and white.
The leaden sea ebbs back, the sky is not yet light.
Hidden from dawn's grey patch
Behind frosted windows, ash ticks out faded hearths.

How quickly time passes. There is no mark
Yet upon this manuscript of snow.
Where water dripped, ice glitters, sheaved and stark.
The pen has fallen from the hand of dark.
White are lintel and latch.
Earth has forgotten where her dead go.

Silence. Then a curlew flutes with its cry
The low distance, that throbbing Spring call,
Swifter than thought. It is good-bye
To all things not beginning, and I must try,
Making the driftwood catch,
To coax, where the cry fades, fires which cannot fall.

Life and Death

Air

If a man have but one string,
One, on which to play,
Or in all the world one thing
He alone can say,

Let him turn to other kinds,
Lose and find himself,
Find the peace another finds,
Never for himself.

Music is of music wrought,
Silent though it stay.
Stretch the string away from thought
And the string will play.

Second Air

After all is said,
Then the words alone
Keep a single thread,
Yes, one tone.

Perfect music is
What it had to be:
Wit, the gift of grace,
Bound, yet free.

Everything is caught,
Singular and glad;
Then the after-thought,
Though not sad,

Leads us to a plain
Where the stream is dry,
And we hear again
That low sigh

Earth has breathed who hears
After all is said,
One with many tears
Still unshed.

Two Sources of Life

The time we measure and the time we know
Move in the branches drinking life, the giver.
Being young, we bathed here, and shook off the river,
Then stood above the stream and watched it flow.
An image in the water shone below,
Armed with a secret we could not deliver.
Those beams were like the arrows in a quiver
For which our expectation was the bow.

But ask: when was it that the current took us
So deeply into life that time forsook us,
Leaving us nothing but the need to give?
We were tranfigured by the deaths of others.
That was the spring, when first we knew our brothers
And died into the truth which made us live.

Triads

Who am I to load the year with continual misunderstanding?
I will not accuse winter of a protracted hardness,
Nor spring of callousness, nor summer of regret.

The oak-leaf changes: green gloss cups the acorn.
First hidden, then emerging from resistance to statement,
The fruit holds nothing in its fullness but the tree.

To have held through hail, stormwinds, and black frost in
      darkness
Through the long months, gives meaning to the bud when it
      opens.
Song loses nothing of moments that are past.

So my labour is still: it is still determination
To resolve itself slowly in the weathers of knowledge.
By virtue of the hidden the poem is revealed.

Remember Earth's triads: the faith of a dumb animal,
The mountain stream falling, music to the wheat-ears;
The salt wave echoing the grieving of the bones.

The lamb leaps: it is stubborn in its innocence.
The hawk drops, in the energy of instinct.
Dawn fires kindle perfection like a sword.

Fires: the hawk's talons, the tongue of the chameleon,
In a peacock's wings' lightning the contraction of glory,
In death the last miracle, the unconditional gift.

What do I need but patience before the unpredictable,
The endurance of the stepping-stone before the footprint,
Cadence that reconciles wisdom and the dance?

I need more, I need more. In the moment of perception
Fit me, prayer, to lose everything, that nothing may be lost.
The stone that accumulates history is falling.

History is a pageant, and all men belong to it.
We die into each other: remember how many
Confided their love, not in vain, to the same earth.

Fisherman

I learn, as my fingers mend the net, what none without nets
    can know.
The sun of that knowledge flickers within. It is not the knotting
    of cords;
It is not the silent pull on the net, the pull of the sea, when the
    flow
Carries the weight of an unknown tide, when the heart is laden
    with words.

How many tides have ebbed and flowed where pebble and
    broken shell
Shine in a tumbled spangle of weed: O little weights of the
    mind,
O little floats to carry me up in a moment none can foretell,
We are taken, each, by the task we choose, by the net our
    hands designed.

There are silver fish that flash before day, in the fragile moment
    of dawn.
I have seen them shiver before my eyes, then vanish before
    light shone.
I know the weight of unspoken words, of speech that cannot
    be drawn.
I crouch, and my life returns to the sea. It trembles, then it is
    gone.

Fingernail Sunrise

The salt wave sings
Before, beyond, and under time, and along the long sand falls,
Dinted with brilliant things
Coiled or broken, deaf to the wild birds' calls.

Pause, and look down.
The flash we saw in the distance now becomes for us a shell,
Spun from the loom of waters to its own
Stillness, and inward music: mark it, where it fell.

Stilled at the core
Of sky and water, skimmed by shag and oystercatchers flown,
Leaving the print of talons on the shore
Of daylight, and the shore of all that's known:

Thought ends in this.
A hundred footprints now arrive at this fine skin of horn
Divining daybreak here by artifice,
Fingernail sunrise, rifted sky reborn.

Should a man die,
Leaving a fingered skein, though never of this workmanship,
Certain and cold, and be outlasted by
Such art, who then might hear the speaking lip,

Unseen, confess:
'Here, in the heart of colour, in the tidewrack of the sea,
 This mask of mine, for winds to dry and waters to caress,
 Shuts history out, till turned by its own key?'

The half is written,
Split like a shell, silvered with pearl, now death has overlaid it,
Secret, beautiful, and forgotten,
Mute, remembered alone by him who made it.

Fidelities

The fountain gathers, in a single jet,
Fidelities where beams together run,
Thrives upon loss, enriches us with debt.

Nothing will match the day's full unison.
I love to see light break; and yet, and yet,
The final arbiter is not the sun.

Bounteous that brother, but he will forget
Others whose eyes the hand of death has closed,
Nor touch, nor seek them, when their light has set.

Seeing of what compound splendour life's composed,
Who could believe it now a part once played,
With so much owing to so many a ghost?

Of love's stern language noblest lives are made.
The shell of speech by many a voice is shot
Whose light, once kindled, cannot be betrayed.

A certain cadence underlies the plot;
However fatally the thread is spun,
The dying man can rise above his lot.

For me neglect and world-wide fame were one.
I was concerned with those the world forgot,
In the tale's ending saw its life begun;

And I was with them still when time was not.

Notes

WALES

Waterfalls: from *Affinities*

1 "That valley in Wales": Taff's Well, Glamorgan, the home of VW's paternal grandfather.

The Broken Sea Section 9: from *The Lamp and the Veil.*

Section 9 of a poem in 20 sections, written for the poet's godchild' Danielle Dufau-Labeyrie, born in Paris, May 1940. VW was to have flown to Paris for her baptism, but was prevented from going by the fall of France. The poem moves continually between Paris and Swansea, both at that time under enemy attack.

2 "The bay": Foxhole, Pennard, below the cliff on which VW lived.

7 "St. Mary's": the parish church of Swansea, destroyed by an incendiary raid in February 1941.

11 "Pearl White": the heroine of the silent films which were shown in the Uplands Cinema, Swansea, now Lloyds Bank, where VW used to see them as a child. See 'Elegy on the Heroine of Childhood', *The Ballad of the Mari Lwyd.*

"Cwmdonkin Drive": VW often visited Dylan Thomas in his parents' house, number 5.

15 "The painter of limbo": Alfred Janes, painter, and friend of VW, whose studio was at the top of his father's greengrocery warehouse in Alexandra Terrace, Swansea.

16 "The extravagant hero of night": Dylan Thomas.

39 "Town Hill": a hillside suburb of Swansea which faces West, so that the windows catch the fire of sunset.

The Forge of the Solstice: from *Cypress and Acacia.*

3 "One scrawls on rock": David Jones, painter, poet and maker of inscriptions.

7 "Another": Ceri Richards, artist.

15 "One is mute": Alfred Janes, artist.

Peace in the Welsh Hills: from *Cypress and Acacia.*

This poem was first conceived during a drive from Swansea to Aberystwyth in the early Autumn of 1958.

The Return of Spring: from *The Lady with the Unicorn.*

This poem is about Bishopston Valley, Gower, where the stream goes underground for part of its journey to the sea.

Bishopston Stream: from *Affinities.*

Another poem set in Bishopston Valley. The poet recalls former times when he walked there with his parents. His father's death suggests a parallel with the disappearance of the stream underground.

POETRY AND THE POET

Rewards of the Fountain: from *Affinities.*

Demands of the Muse: from *Affinities.*

A complex form, uncommon in English poetry, in which there is no rhyme, but, after the first verse, a regular pattern of interchanging end-words takes its place.

Demands of the Poet: from *Affinities.*

The Interval: from *Affinities.*

Vine: from *Affinities.*

The Heron: from *The Death Bell.*

The heron is the type of the poet or seer; see Dylan Thomas' poem 'Over Sir John's Hill', in which the same symbol is used.

Swan Narcissus: from *Fidelities.*

Taliesin and the Spring of Vision: from *Cypress and Acacia.*

For the full story of Taliesin see the Mabinogi of Taliesin in Lady Charlotte Guest's translation of *The Mabinogion.* This was VW's source, although in this poem he changes the legend. In the original story, the boy Gwion, who is destined to be reborn as the bard Taliesin, gets the three drops which bring vision from the cauldron of Ceridwen. Here it is the mature poet who is faced with the consequences of the seer's insight.

Muse, Poet and Fountain: from *Affinities.*

The verses are spoken successively by the Muse, the Poet and the Fountain.

DYLAN THOMAS

The Curlew: from *Cypress and Acacia*

Exegesis: from *Fidelities.*

> This poem, like 'A True Picture Restored', was occasioned by the spate of reminiscences about Dylan Thomas after his death, many by acquaintances whose knowledge of him was superficial.

The Sloe: from *Cypress and Acacia.*

> The dream referred to here made a deep impression on VW. He describes it more fully in 'The Exacting Ghost' and 'The Return'. Dylan Thomas is buried in Laugharne.

The Present: from *Affinities.*

> This poem is about a photograph by Rollie McKenna of Dylan Thomas, which VW kept on his writing-table. 'Portrait of a Friend' is about an earlier photograph of Dylan Thomas.

Cwmrhydyceirw Elegiacs: from *Fidelities*

> An earlier poem, 'At Cwmrhydyceirw Quarry', also refers to the occasion when VW and the sculptor Ronald Cour chose the stone for the Dylan Thomas memorial now in Cwmdonkin Park.

Buried Light: from *Cypress and Acacia.*

To a Shell: from *Fidelities.*

> Written on seeing again, after many years, the small house 'Sea View' at Laugharne, in which Dylan and Caitlin Thomas had spent their happiest years, soon after they were married.

The Snow Curlew: from *Fidelities.*

LIFE AND DEATH

Air and *Second Air*: from *Uncollected Poems*.

These poems were found on VW's desk after his death.

Two Sources of Life: from *Fidelities*.

3 See also 'Revisited Waters', section 1, 'The Constant Stream' (*Affinities*) for the imagery of the stream used in this sonnet.

Triads: from *Fidelities*.

Fisherman: from *Fidelities*.

Fingernail Sunrise: from *Fidelities*.

Fidelities: the title poem of *Fidelities*.

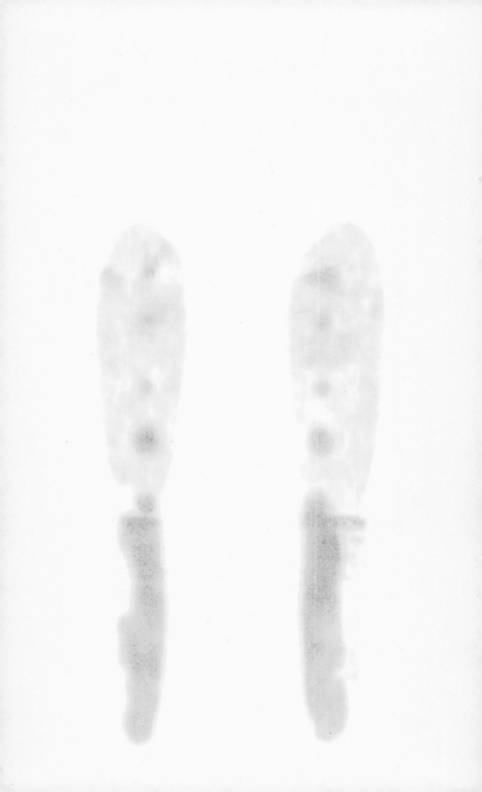

72631

WATKINS, VERNON

L THAT WAS BORN IN WALES

DATE DUE

GAYLORD   PRINTED IN U.S.A.